Fortress of Louisbourg

✤

Text by
JOHN FORTIER

Photographs by
OWEN FITZGERALD

Toronto
OXFORD UNIVERSITY PRESS
1979

This book is dedicated to those who lived in Louisbourg during the eighteenth century, to those who have kept its memory alive, and to those who have re-created it today.

The Publishers wish to thank the staff of the Fortress, without whose total collaboration this book would not have been possible.

Designed by FORTUNATO AGLIALORO

Introduction

The Fortress of Louisbourg stands on a low peninsula of Cape Breton Island that lies between Louisbourg Harbour and the Atlantic Ocean. It was built by the French in the eighteenth century as a walled city close by the historic sea lanes of the North Atlantic. Today, in one corner of the site, it is being reconstructed by the Government of Canada as it appeared during the early 1740s.

It is a visual delight. The lines, shadows, and textures of its European architecture are unavoidably picturesque. Its rugged environs have a dramatic appeal quite apart from the influence they have exerted on history. Many visitors, who expect to find only another palisaded fort in a remote part of the continent, are surprised by the scale of the place and to discover that its role in history is greater than they realized.

Even before its brief heyday had ended, Louisbourg was something of a legend, a place where history was played out on a scale larger than life. From its founding in 1713, it quickly became the third busiest seaport on the continent, after Boston and Philadelphia. The philosopher Voltaire called Louisbourg 'the key' to French possessions in North America. Searching for words to describe its strategic importance, many have called it the 'Gibraltar of the North', and the 'Dunkirk of America'. Alarmed by this spectacular manifestation of French power, the British eyed Louisbourg covetously. 'No care or expence [sic] can be thought too great for the preservation of it; nor any equivalent sufficient for the loss of it,' one writer was to declare in 1749.

Far from being an isolated 'outpost', then, Louisbourg was a centre of military and commercial activity in the North Atlantic. Much closer to Europe, and much more accessible by ship, than the scattered French settlements up the St Lawrence, its well-defended harbour was one of the most secure in the New World. As a fishing base, its harvest from the sea – mainly codfish – was far more valuable to the economy of France than the fabled fur trade of the interior.

As a naval port, Louisbourg was destination and shelter for a large fleet of French warships, merchantmen, and fishing vessels that came out from Europe each spring. It had one of the first lighthouses in North America (an impressive tower that burned down shortly after it was completed and was rebuilt to be fireproof). Its careening wharf, naval hospital, harbour pilots, signal system, Admiralty Court, King's stores, forges, and bakery made it one of the most complete anchorages on this side of the Atlantic.

As an entrepôt of commerce, it drew ships from Europe, the West Indies, Québec, Acadia, and New England. Its wharves and warehouses were crowded with fish for export, merchandise for trans-shipment, and a vast range of imports to sustain the colony. Louisbourg lived by trade. The town made or grew very little of its own necessities, and when the transports failed to arrive, the fortress experienced hardship and even famine.

The town was home to a garrison of 600 soldiers in the 1740s (increased to 3,500 in the 1750s), and a permanent population of some 2,000 administrators, clerks, innkeepers, artisans, fishermen, and their families. As capital of the colony of Ile-Royale, its jurisdiction extended over the outports on all of Cape Breton and Prince Edward islands, although to a great degree Louisbourg *was* Ile-Royale.

In its attachment to European customs, Louisbourg developed in a pattern different from the rest of New France. Following the style of many walled cities in France, it was built according to a regular grid plan – one of the first in North America. Its wide, straight streets, impressive town gates, and vistas focused on its principal buildings, reflect a typically European attitude of permanence. The absence of seigneurial estates, and of almost any kind of farming or agrarian activity, prevented the emergence of a landed aristocracy. Instead, the free grants of land to fishermen and merchants, and the ample opportunities to get rich by trade and speculation, created a strong merchant class based on commerce and money-making. Louisbourg's commercial ties with New England, some of them illicit but apparently profitable for both sides, were as important as its ties with the other colonies of France.

Compared with the rest of the New World, Louisbourg was urbane and sophisticated. News and fashions from France usually reached the colony considerably before the rest of the continent. Louisbourg's senior administrators were veteran naval officers who had travelled widely, commanded warships in battle, and served in the far-flung colonies of France. The resident corps of military engineers, hydrographers, and map-makers – among the best in their profession during the eighteenth century – were highly trained products of the Enlightenment. Dur-

ing the 1750s they established on the walls of the King's Bastion what may have been the first astronomical observatory in North America.

Louisbourg was not a pious place by eighteenth-century standards. Its boomtown rush of military construction, fishing, and commerce, followed by the tumult and destruction of two wars, kept the clergy from exerting the influence they had elsewhere in New France. Some worthy Recollet fathers, and a handful of intrepid sisters of the Congregation of Notre Dame, brought a certain religious presence to the town's highly temporal affairs, while the Brothers of Charity, much less admired by their contemporaries, ran the large and well-appointed hospital, one of the first in North America when it opened in the late 1720s.

In Louisbourg's crowded streets – swollen by the ships' crews, fishermen, and merchants drawn to the town each summer – the variety of social classes and pursuits would have been striking: privateers and dilettantes, clerks and fishwives, carpenters and stone masons, clergy, orphans, apprentices, soldiers working at odd jobs to augment their pay, women of 'bad life', and garrison officers longing for the refinements of France. As in any seaport, the waterfront inns and cabarets were host to a mixture of nationalities and talents: deserters from the armies of Europe sent over as hired soldiers in the Swiss Karrer regiment; Basque and Portuguese fishermen; Dutch and Irish sailors; merchants from some of the largest trading firms in New England; Indian *domestiques*; and West Indian slaves, one of whom became the town executioner (the King bought him a wife as companion in a most unpopular job).

The Fortress of Louisbourg is to be restored partially so that future generations can thereby see and understand the role of the fortress as a hinge of History. The restoration is to be carried out so that the lessons of History can be animated.
Decision of the Federal Cabinet of Canada, 1961

Louisbourg was a town doomed in part by its own success, for while it stood, the fortress excited awe and envy. Its defences were barely complete when an expedition of New England volunteers captured it in an improbable siege in 1745. Against this nest of papists and privateers, they organized their expedition with a mixture of religious fervour and commercial cunning. Louisbourg had become a rival for trade and territory too powerful to ignore.

From its early years the fortress was fatally flawed by its poor location, surrounded by hills, and by its poor construction, which required endless repairs. In spite of these disadvantages, however, it was still a difficult place to attack. Writing to his brother at the beginning of the expedition, Benjamin Franklin warned: 'Fortified towns are hard nuts to crack; and your teeth have not been accustomed to it.' But crack it they did, after a siege that lasted seven weeks. Jubilant, and probably inebriated, the conquerors marched in through the Queen's Gate, accompanied by the dubious music of trumpets, flutes, and violins. Disaster awaited them. During their first winter in the battered town, the victors lost 900 dead and were forced to bury the corpses under the floorboards of their houses until the ground thawed. The wretched garrison mutinied and sought oblivion in drink; when the new military governor arrived with two British regiments raised to relieve the colonials, he ordered the rum confiscated and 64,000 gallons were seized.

When the diplomats traded Louisbourg back to the French in 1748, the newspapers and pulpits of New England reverberated with rage and indignation. A generation later the experience gained at Louisbourg, applied by some of the veterans who had fought there, would be turned against the British in the American Revolution.

Through the 1750s the French toiled continuously to repair and modify the fortress, but they could not overcome the disadvantages of its location. In 1758 a force of 15,000 British soldiers, supported by over 150 ships, captured the fortress as a prelude to the assault up the St Lawrence River against Québec.

After the fighting was over, General Wolfe remarked, with characteristic acerbity: 'If it had been attacked by anybody but the English, it would have fallen long ago.' Yet the conquest of Ile-Royale was a shattering blow to the French. Soon after the first siege a requiem for the fortress was written by Governor Charles Knowles, who had served there (and detested the place): 'Upon the whole, the General design of the Fortifications is Exceedingly Bad and the Workmanship worse Executed and so Disadvantageously Situated that almost every rising Ground or little Eminence Commands one part or other, that either a Vast Sum of money must be laid out to Fortifye it properly or it will never answer the Charge or Trouble.'

By 1760, with British control firmly established over the continent and a much stronger military base

To those of us whose minds work that way it is fascinating, even compelling, to stand at the edge of an archaeologist's trench at Louisbourg and watch the detritus of history – boards, bricks, trash, cannon-shot, the rubble of homes and households – being exposed. It would be rash, and peculiar to our twentieth-century preoccupation with details, to assume that we can better understand our ancestors merely by poring over their garbage. Yet more emerges from Louisbourg than simply an accumulation of research data or the shells of buildings as we imagine they existed.

growing up in Halifax, Louisbourg was no longer needed. British miners tunnelled into its ramparts and blew them up – a dramatic end to a dramatic place. Its wealth and its weakness had made Louisbourg a flashpoint for imperial rivalry, and had twice kindled the wars that finally engulfed the French colonies in North America. Countless fortunes, careers, and lives were wagered at Louisbourg, and many were lost there. So much depended on its fate that it was truly 'a hinge of history'. The fall of Louisbourg was one of the critical events that determined whether the continent would develop under French or British influence; the consequences of that decision by arms remain with us still.

Many of the redcoats who would fight in the Revolution had participated in the second siege, and some stayed to garrison Louisbourg for a decade afterward. They finally left behind a town that was heavily damaged but never entirely abandoned. A handful of discharged soldiers and fishermen continued to eke out an existence among the ruins, and their descendants can still be found in the present town of Louisbourg. At the close of the Revolution they were joined by a party of Loyalists, led by the former mayor of Albany, New York, who soon moved on to found the city of Sydney.

For years the shattered fortress was a source of cutstone and hardware for buildings as far away as Halifax. Eventually all that could be seen of the old walls were several casemates of the King's Bastion; with their ends destroyed, they looked like tunnels and became a landmark during the nineteenth century. Sheep grazed on the mounded walls and in the craters left by the demolition of 1760. Strewn around the harbour bottom were the remains of a fleet of French warships sunk during the siege. The most casual visitor could discover some artefact as a souvenir: broken dishes, cannon shot, buckles, nails, bricks, even bones washed out along the beach. The ruins were a tempting place for historians of the nineteenth century to visit and contemplate the sweep of history, as did Francis Parkman:

This grassy solitude was once the 'Dunkirk of America;' the vaulted caverns where the sheep find shelter from the rain were casemates where terrified women sought refuge from the storms of shot and shell, and the shapeless green mounds were citadel, bastion, rampart and glacis. Here stood Louisbourg; and not all the efforts of its conquerors, nor all the havoc of succeeding times, have availed to efface it.... The remains of its vast defences still tell their tale of human valor and human woe.

History is usually written by the victors, who readily come to assume that their success was preordained. There has long been a widespread assumption that the fall of Louisbourg and the collapse of New France were inevitable and so to be taken for granted. Research for the reconstruction at Louisbourg has shed new light on the importance of the fortress and refutes some old ideas about the place. In carrying out this research Louisbourg's historians have undergone a subtle shift of perspective.

Much has been said, for example, about the reputation of Louisbourg as a disastrous drain on the treasury of France. A remark is often attributed to King

A scheme adequate to introduce new wealth into Cape Breton and bring fresh and heightened scenes and an evaluation of mind and spirit to its people . . . a comprehensive representation of the material and cultural forms set up in a strange land inviting settlement.
Justice I.C. Rand, Report of the Royal Commission on Coal (1960)

Louis XV that some day he expected to see the towers of Louisbourg looming on the horizon. We have yet to discover that comment in a document written at the time, probably because the King got a bargain at Louisbourg. Given the fortune in fish to be hauled out of the waters around Ile-Royale, and the need to protect French territory in the North Atlantic, the construction of the fortress, even in its most expensive year, never cost more than the outfitting of a large warship for a summer voyage from France and back. Instead of a single ship posted in these dangerous waters, France got a base for its navy and fishing fleets and a thriving city that returned much wealth to the empire.

Although much has been written about the vulnerability of Louisbourg as a fortress in the two sieges, the British and the New Englanders long regarded it as a glorious conquest. Another viewpoint has been offered by French historians in Québec, who speak of Louisbourg as a success because it defended the Gulf of St Lawrence and delayed the fall of Canada. Both views ignore the fate of the garrison and colony that the fortress was supposed to protect in the first instance.

In the eighteenth century and until the reconstruction began, the common image of Louisbourg, derived from engravings, was that of a place being attacked: the viewpoint was that of a besieger. After coming to know the original inhabitants of Louisbourg almost as well as we know our own friends and neighbours, we now see the fortress not as besiegers but as townspeople and defenders. In this light we can only conclude that the fortress was a failure. Although no fortress was expected to hold out for more than a few weeks without reinforcements, it was expected to shield the buildings and people inside from enemy cannon. On this basis Louisbourg failed miserably.

The destruction of the fortress made Louisbourg a graveyard in its own time, but preserved it for us in a way that no one could have anticipated. The ruins that have survived virtually untouched from the eighteenth century are among the most evocative on this continent. As an archaeological site of rare completeness, Louisbourg is the only major colonial town in North America that does not have a modern city built on top of it. The past is very close both physically and emotionally.

There are few historic sites where the importance of the terrain and climate can so easily be seen through their impact on the events that happened there. In some significant ways this has been enhanced by the reconstruction of the fortress. Standing on the walls of the demi-bastion Dauphin one can see, even feel, how the hills outside commanded the fortress, made it an 'amphitheatre' and such a wretched place to defend. The now-reconstructed powder magazine, whose walls stood through two sieges and lay buried for two centuries after the demolition, is a battered testimony to the unexpected changes brought by time. The wet chill visitors experience made the fortress difficult to build and repair; it explains the short building season and why so many of the garrison and townspeople turned to drink – if only to keep warm. The fog and storms that overwhelm the place create a sense of awe for the perils that were routine to the early sailors and settlers of the North Atlantic.

That site marks a salient occasion in the transplantation of a civilization significant to the history of Canada; and to allow it to sink into ruin and obliteration would be a grave loss to the civilizing interests of this country.
Justice I.C. Rand (1960)

Beyond the ruins of the eighteenth-century hospital, Louisbourg rises again.

Louisbourg is a place of many moods. Its climate is strong and dramatic, whether seen in the low wet clouds that filter the sun, the changing colours of the sea, or the frequent fogs that most of us learn to accept (and some even prefer to sunnier weather). This fog is no ordinary mist; at Louisbourg it comes off the sea as large droplets of water, suspended in mid-air and driven before the wind. It can persist for days; at other times it is a moving curtain, anchored offshore, which may obscure one end of the harbour while the other end finds itself in sunshine. From time to time a hurricane comes by. When things get really wet the usual greeting among the people who live there today is 'Dirty weather, eh?', given with an inflection of wonderment from which the casual visitor may conclude that such conditions are relatively rare. Yet if the climate requires a certain stoicism over the long run, it is seldom uninteresting.

To balance the record, it must be said that Louisbourg is not continually fog-bound, in spite of its reputation. This is an exaggeration, arising from the complaints of certain British officers in the eighteenth century, and perpetuated with a feeling of smugness by mainlanders who seldom come near the place. Old-timers believe the situation has changed for the better since the Canso Causeway, opened in 1955, changed the flow of water between Cape Breton and Nova Scotia.

Another myth is that Cape Breton must be very cold in winter – an impression formed by visitors who encounter a chill summer day. In fact, Cape Breton seldom experiences the 'depth of winter' that settles over most of Canada. (Here is where the moist coastal climate evens things out a bit.) There is almost no time during winter when it may not rain instead of snow, then freeze, then thaw, then do something else. Louisbourg's climate in winter is much like that of Halifax or Boston; in the summer, much like that of Newfoundland.

After ten years in Louisbourg, my predominant impression is of the wind: that is the one constant element all year round. The wind is so strong and persistent that it stunts and shapes the spruce trees growing along the coast; so fundamental to life in this area that it is the main means of predicting weather. On the mainland, people look at the clouds to forecast weather; but here the fishermen, whose livelihood depends a great deal on knowing the sea and the weather, have always read their signals in the wind.

Back when every ship moved by sail, a steady breeze was of practical value. The French who settled Louisbourg chose this harbour because it was a short sail to the fishing banks. They might sink in a gale, or be driven on the rocks – a fate that even the most experienced mariners sometimes could not avoid – but they would seldom sit idle because they found themselves becalmed.

Louisbourg is a place where the sea and wind seem to challenge the land and the people on it. It is impossible to stand near Black Rock or Lighthouse Point when the surf is up and not share the feelings of one observer, who remarked:

It is singular that this point, exposed to the continual fretting, dashing and ebullition of this particularly restless sea, and placed at the mercy of every storm that sweeps the Atlantic, should yet bear so little evidence of its power.

Louisbourg Harbour, and the eastern tip of Cape Breton, sit on the remains of a volcano that was active more than 500 million years ago. The molten rock that formed this rugged coastline will stand up to the surf for a long time, but the sea may be winning anyway. Archaeological research on the eighteenth-century quay wall has revealed that the water level has risen – or, to be more precise, that the land has subsided – by eighteen inches during the last two centuries. The reconstructed wharves and gates in the fortress have been raised so that they still meet the water at the same relative height. We can merely

hope that centuries from now Louisbourg will not have become an underwater legend, like Atlantis.

The same implacable wind and sea and climate have always given the fortress site a feeling of isolation, and even timelessness. For many years it has seemed that here was a compelling place to tell not only the turbulent history of the struggle between the French and English, but also the fascinating and little-known story of the society that briefly flourished at Louisbourg and then was extinguished by military conquest.

The fortress was given its first scholarly study by Senator J. S. McLennan, a local coal-company executive who became fascinated with the place and in 1917 published *Louisbourg: From its Foundation to Its Fall*, which is still the most comprehensive book on the subject. The trust was carried on by his daughter Katharine, who saw the federal government extend its protection over the site in 1928 and build a museum there in the 1930s. For many years Katharine was the curator, and also the benevolent and proprietary moving spirit behind the commemoration of eighteenth-century Louisbourg and its people.

In 1960, with the future of the Cape Breton coal mines in serious doubt, the Royal Commission on Coal, chaired by the Honourable I. C. Rand, recommended a number of responses by the government. One of these was to reconstruct the fortress. Like many others who had visited the ruins at Louisbourg, Rand came away convinced of their importance: 'That site marks a salient occasion in the transplantation of a civilization significant to the history of Canada; and to allow it to sink into ruin and obliteration would be a grave loss to the civilizing interests of this country.'

Realizing the undesirable aspects of Cape Breton's dependence on a single industry, Rand's report called for alternative economic and cultural activities – 'a scheme adequate to introduce new wealth into Cape Breton and bring fresh and heightened

scenes and an elevation of mind and spirit to its people.' With great far-sightedness, Rand predicted the social benefits that could be realized from his short-term solution to an economic problem. 'For too long has the Island been put down as a bleak mining region,' he argued.

Here are resources of profundity as well as of enjoyment; the scenes are a national property to be brought to an attainment of their potentialities. What is proposed will be not only of economic benefit to the Island; it will introduce elements to regenerate its life and outlook, dissolve the climate of drabness and let into human hearts and intelligence the light of new interests, hopes and ambitions. Mechanical industry remains uncertain, but there are pursuits of deeper purpose lying within the will and action of people and governments.

'What could be more stimulating to the imagination or instructive to the mind,' the report concluded, than a reconstruction of the fortress that would give 'a comprehensive representation of the material and cultural forms set up in a strange land inviting settlement.'

In 1961 the federal government authorized the beginning of a 25-million-dollar program to rebuild part of the fortress and town and re-create a historical cross-section of the military, maritime, commercial, administrative, and civilian activities that originally existed in Louisbourg. Approximately 225 men, mostly former coal miners, were put to work, learning new trades and eventually moving on to other jobs. Although the labour force is now much smaller, a few are still with the fortress. They are joined each summer by a corps of guides and service staff that puts Louisbourg's seasonal employment total well over 300. When the reconstruction is finished in the 1980s, visitors will be able to wander the eighteenth-century waterfront, explore the fortifications of Louisbourg's landward defences, or lose themselves in the barracks, 365 feet long, once the largest building in New France.

Unlike many outdoor museums, which consist of buildings installed in an artificially created setting, Louisbourg has been reconstructed on its original site. This gives the work an interest, but also creates problems, that the other places do not have. Before reconstruction could begin, the area had to be excavated by archaeologists – a process that cannot be rushed without losing the unique information implicit in the build-up of layers of human occupation. In the process of uncovering this evidence, much of it is destroyed, so that analysis has to be done carefully, and a choice has to be made between preserving ruins untouched and digging them up for the information they can yield. At Louisbourg most of the ruins of the fortifications and town will remain undisturbed. In silent contrast to the bustling reconstruction, they are a powerful reminder of how completely Louisbourg was destroyed.

It has been difficult to install modern foundations and utilities while still preserving fragments of the archaeological site. Yet certain buildings have been reconstructed on their original walls, and certain features, such as wells and cobblestone paving, survive just as they were found. It remains difficult, on this historic ground, to accommodate the annual surge of visitors and the modern activities that are part of operating a major tourist attraction – in themselves nearly as complex as in any town where people live – without losing sight of the archaeological features and the need to preserve them for future generations. It is necessary at times to remind both visitors and staff that the reconstruction is not an end in itself, merely a point of departure from which to understand and explain the past. The historic site has its own sombre story to tell, and we do history an injustice if our own comings and goings in this remarkable place ever obscure it.

If the reconstruction lacks the intangible appeal of original buildings, it still can claim to be as valid as the historical districts that have been rebuilt in the old cities of Europe after their destruction in the Second World War. Although Louisbourg lay in ruins for a longer period, it has been resurrected for similar reasons – to recall the past and preserve a focus for our heritage.

As a student of the past, I think the great challenges and rewards of working at Louisbourg have come from taking an enormous mass of historical and archaeological evidence and turning it into a physical result that people can experience and enjoy. It is hoped that they will gain a greater appreciation of the historic site and the events that happened there, for as one writer has declared: 'If there are any historic sites of the first magnitude in North America, few can justly lay claim to greater importance.' None has greater potential to illustrate the lessons of history, and few have been developed so intensively for that purpose.

Unlike many museum villages that present a twenty- or thirty-year span of time, Louisbourg is reconstructed to a very specific era: the early 1740s. It had to be. Before that time the military construction and many of the private buildings were not finished; after 1745 they had been damaged in the siege and had entered a period of repairs and modifications that would be very difficult to portray. Guides and visitors alike experience a milieu poised between peace and war, one that was soon to be ended. The military undertone is restrained, in order to focus attention on the life that filled the town. There are restored forts all across the continent where soldiers drill relentlessly and fire off enormous quantities of black gunpowder. This rarely happens at Louisbourg: here the emphasis is on the administrative routine of the garrison and its domestic activities.

For years people have thought only of the fortress and forgotten there was a town. Now, in depicting the diversity and wholeness of the community that flourished at Louisbourg, we see the fortress more as being the frame for the picture. To further explain the place and its people, and present the wealth of information that lies behind the reconstruction, various historic buildings are being used for exhibits.

There is much to tell. Most restorations have problems arising from lack of evidence. At Louisbourg the problem has been an abundance of evidence, some of it contradictory. Figuring out what really happened from several different versions is much more difficult than relying on only one source. However, as a result of an extraordinary scholarly effort, the reconstruction possesses a high degree of accuracy. Louisbourg's historians have gathered some 750,000 pages of documents; its archaeologists have excavated dozens of structures and countless artefacts. The results will take several lifetimes to analyse fully, and more information keeps turning up. In the National Archives in Paris recently historians found a magnificent collection of fabric samples, including prices and descriptions of how each was manufactured, compiled by the government during the early 1740s. The variety, quality, and range of colours are stunning and changed many existing ideas about eighteenth-century clothing. At almost the same time as these samples were being preserved, the British navy was capturing French ships at sea and sending the correspondence they carried to London – where it remained unopened until its chance discovery by one of Louisbourg's historians. Breaking the seals on these letters for the first time since they had been written, we found yet another perspective on the past: sheet music, insurance contracts, playing cards, and a plaintive letter from a young man in the colonies wondering why his family had not written for months.

Most outdoor museums depict the people of their locale and tradition. The staff at Louisbourg are learning and demonstrating the skills, customs, and values of a society that is in many respects remote from their own. Except for several communities on the other side of Cape Breton, the French language and culture have disappeared from around Louisbourg just as completely as the walls of the fortress itself. So the job of re-creation is doubly difficult. To complement the reconstruction, Louisbourg's guides and custodians dress in appropriate clothing, and even attempt to portray the lives of specific inhabitants. If our goal is to re-create a real place, it follows that the lives of the original people, as well as the physical environment they knew, are relevant and deserve to be recalled. We know that life in eighteenth-century Louisbourg was arduous and often dreary. The documents make it quite clear that the townspeople were not strangers to high prices, scarcities, illnesses, and disputes. However, these aspects of life can only be implied for visitors. There are limits, after all, to how much we can demonstrate, and it is not 'sugar-coating' the past to respect the bounds of decency and common sense.

Each member of the costumed staff in the reconstructed buildings represents someone – if not an original inhabitant, then at least a specific class of townsperson. A soldier receives the *nom de guerre* of an original soldier and a dossier of historical information on the man so that he may better understand the person he is to represent. The town clock is set

The land between Gabarus point and the town is very uneven, marshy, and full of brambles. It is covered with turf twelve feet deep, which all the art of man can never dry up. Neither is there any possibility of draining off the water, the bogs being surrounded with high rocky ground.
Thomas Pichon, Genuine Letters and Memoirs...of Cape Breton (1760)

according to sun time. The inn and cabaret observe the rules of fast and abstinence established by the Catholic Church during the eighteenth century. Although these things may appear extreme, we have learned that the only way to appreciate history is to begin by taking it seriously and to encourage activity that is relevant to the historical environment, rather than mere posing in costume. The effort itself is significant and can lead to a sympathy with the people we portray, much like that of a biographer for his subject.

At Louisbourg we rely heavily on this form of expression, partly because the town itself is a replica and needs such interpretation and partly because the isolated setting lends itself so well to a re-creation of the past. This approach is a phenomenon of North American outdoor museums. Europeans, surrounded as they are by remnants of their past, find it slightly questionable that we should be striving so hard to re-create an era they feel is too recent to merit such attention. Yet two or three hundred years is about as far back as North Americans can trace the past with much certainty, and we find that 'living history' programs of outdoor museums help to reach an audience full of people who would otherwise have difficulty sensing their place in the continuum of history.

If it is worthwhile to safeguard the natural elements in Canada's national parks for our benefit, education, and enjoyment, or 'just so they will be there', then we should also have in certain well-chosen places a similar kind of cultural preservation. Louisbourg is that kind of place: a cultural set-piece where the passage of time has been minimized and we can examine a historical era in great detail. The outdoor museums, historic parks, and sites of Canada provide islands of aesthetic stability – more or less free from intrusions of the twentieth century – where the styles in architecture, the arts, furnishings, dress, and even behaviour from a specific era can be assembled and examined in context. Besides being more enjoyable than traditional museums, they offer a learning experience whose full potential we are only beginning to appreciate.

The need exists. In the United States, where the effects of change have been more profound and of longer duration than in much of Canada, historical villages and districts are coming to be regarded as surrogate hometowns that contain a familiar and reassuring landscape for people whose points of reference elsewhere have been altered beyond recognition. Some writers have predicted that historical enclaves may provide a psychological refuge from the pressures of a complicated existence: in the simpler environment offered by asylums of the past, people can renew themselves until they are ready to cope with the uncertainties of life. Whatever its role becomes in the future, Louisbourg and other reconstructions like it will never cease to provide a striking point of comparison between the past and the present.

Our effort at Louisbourg is a new and uncertain one, enacted in a town that is still being rebuilt at one end. We have no illusions that visitors will really think they have left the twentieth century; in any case,

In summer the fields are crowded with Angelica. This long-stalked plant survives from the gardens of the eighteenth century. The French imported it from Europe, using it as a medicinal herb. It is also possible to make candy from the stalk. Like several less-dramatic species of vegetation, Angelica is a silent sentinel marking the former settlements of the French in Cape Breton.

our purpose is to inform people, not trick them. Beyond that, we hope the physical setting will move visitors to think about the things we have in common with our ancestors, whoever they were, wherever they lived. Such an evocation of the past is a momentary thing; it may last no longer than the creaking of a door or the sight of a costumed figure at the end of a street.

Perhaps a moment out of time is all anyone wants, for a gulf between past and present remains in spite of all that we have done, and few visitors would really wish to cross it. At best, life in the past was full of discomforts and uncertainties. Even now, Louis-bourg is an uncomfortable place to visit, yet one that will reward the persistent visitor with a rare feeling that here the past is not only very close but has something important to tell us.

The images that follow show the fortress in all seasons and in many moods. They reveal some of its complexity and visual magnificence. They provide a candid album of our family of guides and volunteers who work so hard to depict the past. They suggest how much life remains the same from age to age, in spite of all the differences that separate us from our ancestors. Most of all they help us to discover and appreciate the heritage that is our own.

JOHN FORTIER

The *Casernes*, or barracks, built across the rear of the King's Bastion to create a citadel, was once the largest building in New France, if not all of North America. Nearly 365 feet long, it was completed in the early 1730s. The *pavillon* (foreground) provided the official *apartement* for the governor of Ile-Royale and his servants. Beyond were rooms for officers, although most moved into houses in the town. The tall windows mark the *Chapelle Saint-Louis*. The drawbridge and ditch allowed the barracks to be defended even against an enemy in the town, and soldiers on the upper floor could sweep the palisade and glacis with musket fire. Approximately 500 soldiers occupied the far half of the *Casernes*. A bakery, and an armoury originally installed in the room below the clock tower, were soon moved to another building because this one was so damp. Various governors looked for excuses to move out of their accommodation, but only two succeeded – they took over the house of the military engineer. The colony's chief civil administrator, the *commissaire-ordonnateur*, was more fortunate; he built a large house in town, then sold it to the King as his official residence to avoid living in the *pavillon* planned for him at the far end of the building.

The impressive *horloge*, or clock tower, of the barracks, was designed in 1733, and rebuilt according to the original plan. The clock is operated by a mechanism installed in the 1730s in a church in Barr, France and acquired for the reconstruction. The original bell was described by one New Englander after the siege as 'an Excellent Bell, the Biggest (By far) that Ever I see (altho' we Broke it)'. During the 1960s archaeologists found a fragment of an enormous bell several hundred feet away in one of the yards in Block 2.

The limestone crest represents the Bourbon royal coat of arms. A piece of the original stone was traced back to the original quarry in Mignac, France, which supplied the material for the reconstruction. The stone-cutting was done by artisans working for the fortress.

The entrance is by a large gate, before which is a draw bridge over a small ditch thru the whole building, in passing to which on the lift [sic] hand, the door opens into the King's Chappell, on the right hand into a dungeon, one of which has a greater resemblance of Hell than the other of Heaven....

Descriptions of Louisbourg, 1741

Weather dark and foggy, with raw, cold air; it was tolerably pleasant in the morning, when I went on shore to visit…and observed, that, in walking on the parade, it turned gloomy all of a sudden, and, in the short space of two or three minutes, there came on so heavy a fog, that a person could not know his most intimate acquaintance at the distance of a very few yards; this exceeded any thing of the kind I ever saw to the westward of Nova Scotia.

Captain John Knox, An Historical Journal…(1769)

In making the barracks a citadel, the French worked to create an 'air de fort' or appearance of strength. Although the garrison might stage a last resistance in such a place, it surrendered in both sieges before events reached so desperate a conclusion. This sortie, guarded by a sentry near the *barrière*, is the only way inside. The guardhouse and its generous porch shelter the town's main guard, located near the *place d'armes* and parade ground.

Guard duty greatly fatigues the soldier, especially in a country as harsh as this one.
Commandant Jean-Baptiste Duquesnel, 1741

Year in and year out, soldiers had to stand guard duty at the fortress. When all the posts were fully manned, as many as one-third of the garrison were mounting guard in 24-hour shifts.

The stairway to this *guerritte* often filled with snow, and sometimes the sentry change would have to wait while the soldiers shovelled through the drifts. In the summer guard duty was easier, but in the damp climate it was seldom comfortable.

Beyond the ditch and palisaded outer defences of the fortress, sheep graze on the glacis. Like their ancestors, they remain oblivious to it all.

Maintenance is a constant problem for artillerymen. This cannon at the King's Bastion is mounted *en barbette* – above the wall, so it can fire in a wide arc wherever an enemy may appear. The soldier in the red uniform is a member of the garrison's Company of Cannoneers-Bombardiers; the other is in the uniform of the troops of the Marine. Soldiers often were assigned to help with the cannon, and the heftier they were, the better. Each barrel weighs 6,600 pounds, and the heavy wood carriage adds nearly another ton in weight.

Homes of officiers and merchants line the streets between the citadel and the waterfront. Each has a fenced yard behind, usually enclosing a garden, well, and outbuildings. The high fences were mainly to discourage theft.

In the foreground are the ice-house, with its cone-shaped roof, and the garrison woodyard.

Across the harbour is the twentieth-century town of Louisbourg. Now, as in the past, it still looks to the sea for its livelihood.

28

In a view almost reversed from the one preceding, the barracks imparts its usual sense of solidity as it looms over the backyards nestled against the fortifications.

Everywhere in this garrison town can be felt a regularity and attitude of permanence, from the tolling of the town clock to the predictable rhythms of the soldiers' day.

The *fleur de lys*, which crowns various buildings in stone or iron, indicates royal ownership. Until the siege, most inhabitants saw in it a symbol of military power and security. Surrounded by the most elaborate defences on the continent, few could have guessed how completely Louisbourg would be destroyed.

29

Sunlight forms patterns on the streets and rooftops; each hour the lines and shadows change.

The most common types of construction are all seen here. The Engineer's residence, on the right, is solid masonry. This expensive style was reserved mainly for King's buildings.

The framed timber house (*left*), is *charpente* with masonry fill. The storehouse of upright logs is built *en picquet*; it is the most modest type of construction, and the only one that originated in North America. The storehouse and homes farther down the street are *charpente* frame with board siding. Much of Louisbourg's building materials, including 'Boston boards' for siding, were imported from New England.

Homes, storehouses, and the cabaret line the Rue Toulouse from the Porte Frédéric to the parade ground. Patches of cobblestone sidewalk, and unpaved roadways, are typical of Louisbourg streets.

I cannot dismiss my remarks on Nova Scotia, without observing, that the fogs, which are almost perpetual here, and farther to the eastward, are certainly to be attributed to the swamps, bogs, lakes, creeks, and innumerable rivers, great and small, that intersect the country everywhere...Some people have adopted a different opinion, imputing them rather to the steamy breath of the vast quantities of fish and sea animals wherewith these coasts and waters abound; but I rather ascribe the great salubrity of the air to the myriads of venomous reptiles and insects that absorb the noxious vapours...

Captain John Knox, An Historical Journal...(1769)

...and yet, Thomas Pichon, writing in 1760, found that:

The streets are wide and regular; and near the principal fort or citadel there is a handsome parade. To the north side of the town there are three gates, and a spacious quay. They have likewise constructed a kind of bridge, called in the French language calles, *which project considerably into the sea and are extremely convenient for loading and unloading of goods.*

In the doorway of the King's *Magazin*, a sentry keeps watch over a shipment of barrels. The Porte Frédéric and its wharf, beyond, provide the town's principal entrance from the harbour.

This island is therefore a kind of center-point to all the rest, as well English as French settlements. And as it is a place of strength, and lies amidst the fishing countries ... most conveniently for protecting all our trade, and annoying that of the enemy, no care or expence can be thought too great for the preservation of it; nor any equivalent sufficient for the loss of it.

William Bollan, The Importance and Advantage of Cape Breton (1746)

At the drawbridge of the Porte Dauphine, a sentry waits to inspect visitors. The slotted openings in either face of the wall allow soldiers in the guardrooms to fire towards the bridge. The limestone crest and trophies are copied from original stones recovered from the ditch.

A detachment of soldiers, commanded by a sergeant carrying a 'partisan', marches out from the Porte Dauphine to meet an important visitor to the town. The drummer wears the King's livery – an elaborate braid which provides identification as well as adornment.

These troops of the Marine – the Navy and colonies were under the same Minister in eighteenth-century France – provided the main garrison forces throughout French North America. They wore a vest of blue and a *justaucorps* of grey-white wool.

Despite the seaborne services in which they had enrolled, symbolized by the white anchor on their leather cartridge boxes, the typical soldier travelled little and was a near-permanent resident of the garrison.

Firing *feux de joie* from a *barbette* – earth mound for mounting cannon – note the ramp.

In 1752 the Governor of Louisbourg celebrated the royal birth of the Duc de Bourgogne. A description of the event finds an echo in the reconstructed fortress.

On Sunday 28th of May this important news was announced at day-break by a salute from all the artillery of the place and the King's ships, the frigates Fidèle *and* Chariot Royal, *which had dressed ship.*

M. le Comte de Raymond gave a dinner to the staff, the engineers, the officers of artillery, and to the other principal officers, to the Conseil Superieur, the Baillage, the Admiralty, and to the ladies of the place.

He had two tables with 50 covers, served in four courses, with as much lavishness as elegance. They drank in turn freely every kind of wine of the best brands, to the health of the King, the Queen, the Dauphin, Mme la Dauphine, M. le Duc de Bourgogne, and to the royal princesses, alternately with the sound of the heavy cannon. This 'symphony' increased the pleasure of the celebration...

At six o'clock, leaving the table, they repaired to the King's Chapel to hear vespers. At the close of the service, the Te Deum was sung to the accompaniment of all the artillery of the town and of the ships. They then went in a procession, as is the custom in the colonies, to the esplanade of the Maurepas gate....

Chapelle Saint-Louis

Drummers on the ramparts
of the King's Bastion.

Officers and lady at the Porte Frédéric.

. . . The governor there lit a bonfire which he had had prepared; the troops of the garrison, drawn up on the ramparts and the covered way, fired with the greatest exactness, three volleys of musketry, and the artillery did the same. After this ceremony, the Governor distributed several barrels of his own wine to the troops and to the public in various locations.

The "Vive le Roi" was so frequently repeated, that no one could doubt that the hearts of the townspeople, the troops, and the country folk, which this festival had attracted, were truly French.

He had given such good orders in establishing continual patrols in command of officers, that no disorder was committed. . . .

About nine in the evening, the governor and all his guests went to see set off the fireworks and a great number of rockets, which he had prepared, and which were very well done.

On his return home, the ball was opened, and lasted till dawn; all kinds of refreshments, and in abundance, were handed round. His house was illuminated with lanterns placed all round the windows, looking on the Rue Royale and the Rue Toulouse.

Three porticoes, with four pyramids, adorned by triple lanterns and wreaths of flowers, rare in such a cold climate, were erected opposite the Rue Royale. . . .

These illuminations were charming in their effect and lasted till the end of the ball; all the houses in the town were also lit up as well as the frigate La Fidèle.

Author unknown, 1752

In a barracks room a soldier cleans his musket. The delicate flintlock firearm was usually his most valuable possession. Although most soldiers were allowed to work for extra pay they were usually impoverished, if not in debt, and owned little besides the clothes they wore and a chest containing a few tools or some hunting gear.

Unless they found lodgings in the town, or were assigned to garrison one of the colony's outposts, Louisbourg's soldiers slept two in a bunk, sixteen per room, in the barracks. Cooking was organized by squads, in the same room. While it lacked many conveniences and afforded no privacy, the relatively new concept of a separate barracks building was probably an improvement over the traditional method of billeting soldiers with civilian families. A large amount of the eighteenth-century soldier's time was taken up by household chores. The spit and polish mentality had only begun to rule military life in Europe, and was far less possible in the wilds of North America.

Most able-bodied soldiers were assigned to work building the fortress or doing odd jobs in town, leaving the unskilled and infirm members of the garrison to stand guard. By working as artisans some soldiers were exempted from military duties for years; and were able to live much like civilians.

Wood is as necessary here as bread.
Governor St Ovide and Commissaire-Ordonnateur De Mézy, 1727

Prudent colonists used every opportunity to store up firewood. The buildings were draughty and the winter long.

This fisherman's house outside the fortress has a sod roof. In spite of the damp climate, it is watertight and reasonably warm.

Louisbourg is a good port, and a safe harbour, and will be sufficiently provided against all attempts made on the same, when the fortifications (about which they incessantly labour) shall be completed. More than an hundred vessels from France arrive every year in this harbour to fish...the cod, which they catch in small craft of the country, and after put into larger vessels, where they salt them, and dry them, from the beginning of June to October, when they all get ready to depart, each one for his assigned port. This island produces some grain: but tho' there are more than four thousand inhabitants, they find their account much better in fishing than in husbandry, and consequently the land lies waste, they procuring all necessaries in exchange for their fish.

Marquis de la Maisonfort, 1732

Although the snow may not come for weeks, a cold wind whips across the fortress while a sentry keeps watch on the *guerritte* of the demi-bastion Dauphin. The postings were two hours in the summer, shortened to one hour in winter.

The face of the bastion was planked after part of the wall collapsed into the ditch. The long season of frost and damp weather bedevilled the builders of the fortress, and created structural weaknesses which they were never able to overcome.

Low clouds driven by a cold wind in autumn create a brilliant pattern of sunlight on rooftops. The cannon of the semi-circular battery point towards Louisbourg harbour. Most of the implements and shot have been stored inside to protect them from the weather; there would be time enough to bring them out should any sails be sighted at sea.

It is another myth about Louisbourg that none of the cannon pointed inland when the siege began. Although the largest guns defended the harbour, and not all the embrasures in the fortress mounted cannon, the artillery were probably as well distributed and effective as the poor location of the fortress would allow.

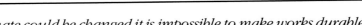

Unless the climate could be changed it is impossible to make works durable, the frosts begin to cease towards the middle of May which are succeeded by foggs, these last till the end of July or beginning of August with the intermission perhaps of one or two fair days in a fortnight, towards the close of September or early in October the frosts set in again and they continue with frequent snow till May or often the beginning of June, so that allowing the fortifications to be repaired with the best of materials and in the most workmanlike manner – Your Grace will observe that they have scarce two months in the year for the cement to dry in, which is impossible for it to do, and therefore it is certain after the Nation has been at the expence of perhaps more than a billion of money we should have to go on again with repairing where we begun at first as it will take upwards of twenty years to do it in and consequently the works be rotten and crumbling down before that time, as they are now.

Governor Charles Knowles, 1746

The harbour of Lewisburg, formerly called the English Harbour,...is perhaps one of the finest in America. It is near four leagues in circumference; and every where there are six or seven fathoms of water. The Anchorage is very good; and you may, without danger, run a ship aground upon the mud.

'In short, there is not in the world a surer retreat for ships, coming from whatever part of America, than Cape Breton, in case of being chased, in case of bad weather, or of want of wood, water, or provisions. Besides, that in time of war, it would be a place...so as entirely to distress the trade of all the British settlements in America.

William Bollan, The Importance and Advantage of Cape Breton (1746)

A circumstance that considerably adds to the horror of this season, is a . . . species of very fine snow, which insinuates itself into every hole and corner, and even into the minutest crevices. It does not seem to fall upon the ground, but to be carried away horizontally by the violence of the wind, so that great heaps of it lie against the walls and eminences; and it hinders a person from distinguishing even the nighest objects, or to open his eyes for fear of being hurt . . . It even takes away one's breath.

Thomas Pichon, Genuine Letters and Memoirs . . . (1760)

The winter is...subject to violent squalls of wind, especially from the south. The sky is generally overcast either with heavy rains, or with thick fogs, especially in summer, which renders it difficult to be discerned at sea. The earth is covered with snow during the winter, and the frost sets in at Christmas...All kind of commerce is then at a stand, and the town puts on a melancholy aspect, very different from the appearance it makes in summer, when crowded with sea-faring people.

Thomas Pichon, Genuine Letters and Memoirs (1760)

Our miserys and distresses occasioned by the severity of the weather I really want words to describe. Nature never seems to have designed this a place of residence for man, for with the poet we may justly say:
     'Here elements have lost their uses
     Air ripens not nor earth produces.'
Governor Charles Knowles, 1747

The severity of the winters, and the want and misery I foresee people in these parts must be exposed to, make me despair of any enterprize succeeding in Accadia or Nova Scotia.
Governor Charles Knowles, 1747

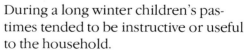

During a long winter children's pastimes tended to be instructive or useful to the household.

The daughter is learning to make lace. (Spinning and weaving were prohibited in the French colonies in order to encourage manufacturing at home.) Sons of officers in Louisbourg usually followed their father's profession by joining a company as a cadet. While his brother plays a jew's harp, the oldest boy learns the proper way to handle a sword.

In the kitchen of the De Gannes house, children at play stack furniture while servants wash the dishes after a meal.

Before they grow much older these children will be expected to help with work around the house, or even take up an apprenticeship in a trade.

The Engineer's living room. Warm weather allows the furniture to be moved away from the fireplace, back to the windows for better light. At this welcome time the entire household opens out.

———————————— ✳

Mme. de la Boulardarie has just dined here; we drank to your health, and she told me you made her so merry that she saw eight candles instead of one. We did not carry things as far.
Governor Augustin de Drucour, 1754

I am a useless member of a society where there is nothing but gambling. I am not in demand as I do not wish to play, and cannot do so. I go out only to pay my respects, and find gaming tables everywhere. I watch the players for a second to two; I sit in an armchair out of decency and this politeness on my part is most boring.
M. Le Courtois des Bourbes, 1756

After leisurely dinners, the gaming table provided recreation for visitors in the Governor's apartment.

Properly speaking they have but two seasons, winter and autumn...
Thomas Pichon, <u>Genuine Letters and Memoirs</u> (1760)

Spring is doubly welcome because it comes so late. A boy tosses a stick while his mother looks over the newly planted garden beds.

The same garden, a few weeks later, has become an important source of food for the De Gannes household.

Mrs. Bastide is very busy about the flower garden, but you never saw such a country. No bright sun, this month past, and what sallade I have had is from ye heat of ye dung and not of the sun.
Captain John Henry Bastide, 1748

During his service in Louisbourg the British military engineer lamented the spring weather. The garden he had is still a difficult place in which to grow anything.

The Engineer's garden, like many others, was laid out in formal patterns, usually symmetrical. Practical as well as ornamental, the plantings were mainly varieties that could be eaten or used for medicine. The stone pedestal in the centre of the garden is a base for a sundial.

A servant prepares a meal in the Engineer's residence. Recipes are taken from early cookbooks. Ingredients are limited to those listed in historical inventories and shipping lists, and available in Louisbourg during the eighteenth century. Cooking on a wood fire requires a good ability to organize, but gives a flavour that cannot be had by any other method.

Across the room another servant finishes a modest lunch. Dishes will be washed in the sink beyond, which drains into the street outside. The drain hole was discovered in the original foundation wall, which was preserved when the house was rebuilt.

Monsieur Joubert wrote in January 1757: 'Il n'y a rien de nouveau ycy depuis mes dernières; nous sommes tous réduits à la sapinette (spruce beer)...' *Sapinette*, a turgid substance tasting like turpentine, was often brewed from spruce boughs for its scorbutic properties. But in this sea-going town, dark West Indian rum was the favourite drink.

The King's Bakery supplied the garrison and the crews of visiting warships. The large, domed brick ovens can produce several hundred loaves per day. Each firing consumes nearly half a cord of wood, making this building one of the few that are usually warm.

However useful Louisbourg may be for commerce, it is certainly not the most agreeable place to live in, since it is damp, cold and foggy. Sometimes even in summer, they don't see the sun for a fortnight.

London Magazine (1746)

While the loaves are in the oven, two of the King's bakers pause to consider the prospects for another day.

The True Character of a Perfect Soldier ought to be:
 Belief in God
 Love of the Sovereign
 Respect for the Laws
 Preference for honour above all pleasures
 and even life itself.
Lemau de la Jaisse (1741)

The soldiers of Ile-Royale generally fell short of the ideal. Yet in spite of many hardships they bore themselves with a soldier's pride. They mutinied in 1744 to protest shortages of firewood and rations, but fought well when Louisbourg was attacked. Much maligned in their own time and by historians, they were condemned to defeat by weaknesses of the fortress that were the fault of their officers, and by a remote, sometimes indifferent, administration in France.

In a *bureau* of the Engineer's residence, an assistant is surrounded by construction plans and surveying instruments.

From 1724 until the siege of 1745 – most of Louisbourg's construction period – the King's Engineer was Etienne Verrier. By training as well as by temperament, he also worked as architect. Dozens of maps and plans for the fortifications and King's buildings were drawn under his supervision, and have been copied from the French archives to guide the reconstruction.

On the table is a plan of the Royal Battery, which was being repaired when the siege began. Verrier convinced a Council of War that the Battery, a mile away from the fortress on the north shore of the harbour, should be abandoned rather than destroyed. Within days the enemy had taken it over and were using its cannon against the town.

Jean-Baptiste Louis le Prévost Duquesnel, the Commandant, had long suffered from ill health.

In 1744 he had ordered expeditions against Canso and Annapolis Royal, which aroused the New England colonies to attack Louisbourg itself the next year. He had seen an uneasy peace give way to war, but he would not see the destruction that followed from his acts.

Duquesnel died at Louisbourg in October. As described in the inventory of his estate, his bed was a *lit à la duchesse*, with serge hangings the colour of flame. He was buried in the chapel of the barracks.

--- ❋

The major is the principal force which moves everything, and upon his effectiveness depends the order or disorder of the system. In effect, it can be said that if he had as many ages as Argus, and as many mouths as Renommée, he would find use for them if he wished to do his duty.

M. de Guignard, Ecole de Mars (1725)

The town major was the highest-ranking military officer in the fortress. He was also a very busy man, responsible in peacetime and in war for the security of the town as well as the daily affairs of the soldiers.

On the balcony of the governor's apartment, he waits to make his daily report on the state of the garrison.

This place is not secure with so small a garrison if it should be besieged.
Louis Du Pont Duchambon, 1744

In 1744 the long-expected war between France and England was officially declared. At the door of the King's *Magazin*, at the Chapel, and at the principal places around the town, a printed *Ordonnance* was posted to notify people in the colony that hostilities were imminent.

At the semi-circular battery, near the demi-bastion Dauphin, a 24-*livre* cannon looms through a gun embrasure. In the siege of 1745, this battery was totally destroyed. Two centuries later, several cannon and a complete set of cut stones for an embrasure were recovered from the debris.

In 1746 Lieutenant John Suttie wrote:
This place can be of no service to England, only an immense expence . . . In my opinion we have a great deal more land than we know what to doe with. We ought to take the best and leave the worste. I wish to God this place had been blown up.

Sir, I am commanded by His Majesty to acquaint you, that, after the most serious and mature deliberation being had, whether it be expedient to maintain, at so great an expence, the fortress at Louisbourg, together with a numerous garrison there, the King is come to a resolution that the said fortress, together with all the works and defences of the harbour, be most effectually, and most entirely, demolished . . . and all the materials so thoroughly destroyed as that no use may, hereafter, be ever made of the same.

William Pitt, Secretary of State, in a letter to Lord Amherst, February 9th 1760

Throughout the summer of 1760, British miners detonated enormous charges of explosives which they had planted deep inside the fortress walls. The central portion of this postern tunnel, used by soldiers to pass through the rampart to the ditch and outer defensive works, survived the demolition. So did many of the cut stones around the doorway at each end. It was an appropriately dramatic end to a dramatic place. Louisbourg became a graveyard and a stone quarry. Yet the completeness of the destruction would ultimately preserve the fortress, and allow it to live again.

⚜